Frankly Clueless

Heather Finton

published 2017 by Northern Undercurrents

ISBN 978-0-9958247-5-1

Celebrating the power
of friendships everywhere,
and most gratefully my own.

That fable
burned its way in
too deep

my ant trudging
all summer

its path
wearing walls
into ground

habitual track.

I hear grasshoppers
singing in sunshine

their music
lighting my work;

let me clamber
out of worn protections
from sand to grass

rub my wings
on each other,
sounding
in brief season.

Love
is always
and

pushing us
past
either or

cajoling
our bigger self
with open arms

to spread wider

where belly softens
into ocean

where all can swim

limitless and

we summarize
as one.

Deep playful
calls

my midriff
knitting earmuffs
as fast as it can

using threads
I have spun daily
for decades

accumulations,
the lint of my importance.

I remember
a game in the woods,
stringing yarn
with wide gaps
in senseless webs
for beauty's sake;

may the needles
rest their clacking,
may I pull freely
in the disentangling

take this string
outside
for no good reason.

Help me to love
all my things

treasure my treasures
with dear tender touch

care for creaky springs
wipe dust

notice with a free heart
all these kindnesses
in form

as if my storehouse
were made of straw

and I can hear
momentum
in a gentle wind.

Let every greeting
sound its note of goodbye

dark and light hues
in each rainbow

my heart
vivid, full spectrum.

All I can do
is not do

sit helplessly
in the thick of it

weeping
with this grin

monstrous
and innocent
and all the shades of grey

a border
for these shimmering rainbows
reflected in clear water

so fleeting.

I inhabit my home
trusting
that my courage
is deeper than my fears

that it rolls inevitably
relentless dawn and darkness

clearing a path
for all this trembling

a welcome hole
in which I fall
eternal.

No comfort
except the softness
of gravity,

a steady pull
of galactic tension

holding me
in motion.

The friction of folks
is what rubs me raw

scraping my zest
so citrus
fills the room

snapping dry twigs
so my spruce
has more to grow on

steeping my rolled stick
in their hot stories
for soft cinnamon.

Alone
I see and imagine
such harmony
and beautiful blends

but need these real encounters
to stir me fresh.

Even this little wind
dissuades me

trees not nearly horizontal
just bending
waving more briskly
than before

my timid heart
cowed
by this unseen force
made visible.

O may I go outside
find the ways
I am paper and string

impermanence
forcing my laugh

fragility of kite.

Hummingbird

I vibrate so fast
almost invisible
darting
between sweetnesses

thank god
for this nectar,
concentrated feeding

slowing me briefly
iridescence perceived

these poems.

I have been resisting
this fog

compelled to look
for clear skies

afraid of getting lost.

May I sink gracefully
into cold damp,
a blind cloud
hampering action

resting by necessity

asleep until I wake.

I long for him
to take the lead
so long as we go
in the direction
I feel we should go

which is nowhere
in particular
and everywhere we can

and rises like a wave
we must surf with precision
and complete abandon

and get soaked
in cold and wet
and taste heat and salt

and laugh
at the hopeless impossibility
of anything else.

Sleepiness and sloth
conspire
with petulance and blame

oh what a fun party
in my place

these resistant blockaders
defying my intention.

Sweepers,
real protrusions
in creative flow,

may I float in deeper currents

not caught.

And she loves
oh she does
all this crazy evolution

intricate interconnection
helping us breathe

thousands of species
tending this home
with breath
and different kinds of shit

and we
who have heads that nod
in the seeing

prostrate
sometimes by choice.

Good girls
waste so much time

waiting for a sign,
invitation
to take space.

Give me instead
a ragged one,
a quirky serration
cutting through

navigating
wild rivers
undammed.

I don't mean
dynamite

or blasting for the sake of sound

false power forced

but give me a hopeless shrug
and strong rudder

time on water.

Walking
the pace of my steps
birthing sensations
forming as words
with steady feet

feeling my rhythm
methodic on ground
while dog acts as melody
bounding

full random
he springs into joy
landing staccato on earth

leaves and breeze
wagging

my lesser exuberance
constrained by habit

neurophysiology
making change
with each press of earth.

All these pungent years

caffeine
and compost

fuelling growth.

Not just home
or team
or all the gently addicted

but hands stretched
across the world

casa with lights on.

Water there and here
and you have been a channel,

a spigot for so much.

- with thanks to Bean North

I am here
yes me with the blotchy face
and hesitant grace

quiet invitations
that sound like whispers

but also me
that lives in all of us
longing to be seen

the me
that calls you in the night
and begs you
to let courage flow

listening at parties
for the sound of your mountain stream
so we can all disrobe
and bathe in your cold cleansing

calling for your wild fire
to warm us all.

Even as I sob
for all the pain of it

the grind of days
rubbing like bone without cartilage

gritting my teeth
until my jaw can no longer laugh

so deeply appreciating
my own courage
that I cry
for the softness in it

even as I gather a friend
who holds space
for my puddle

even when expletives
are my poem

still the Comedienne
brings laughter
to my empty room

depositing a skidsteer load of shit
while ant crawls on my shoulder
to hasten me outside
for the smelly view

my hilarious life.

I have asked
politely

for things
to not get smashed

and still they do

and I restrain
my wail of protest,
injustice.

Let me revel
in the sound
of breaking

hear how life
cracks crystal
with the high notes

feel this knife twist
in my belly
with some glee

still feeling.

Pause
amid your constrictions

feel breeze
in your cage

let the clock
stop
telling you lies

the truth of time
unknown

gap between heartbeats
extending life.

May I embrace
your rage

without my armour

dropping the story
of wounds inflicted

feeling electric stream
neither hot nor cold

energizing love

in no direction

an open alchemy

producing nothing,

invisible gold.

Rain is pouring
on my summer

and when it falls
as snow
is that better?

Or when the sun
pours relentless heat
drying all the leaves?

Questing for perfection,
will I throw away a year
to wait for one day?

Or let the plunging rush
of all this fresh water
touch me now?

Bat-shit crazy

To go
to the cave of my being

sink deeply
in the dark

musty unknowns
familiar

roll around
on bones and muscle

releasing anguish and delight

muttering half-truths

pretend stories

whispers and shrieks
in wobbly flight
echolocation
tapping my nerves…

may guano
feed daylight gardens.

All those tears
wasted

saltwater
trying to make me thirsty
when I licked them away

body pleading
me to notice
raw beauty.

Not nearly ever
enough

today
the hungry ghosts
are fed

and still this longing
to blanket joy
everywhere

succour the world
with the harmony of chaos.

May I keep open
to this raw burning
this wet fire

courage in terror
exulting.

May that which is scared
crawl into light
a wet dog rescued
on the dock

fear rising up
worms seeking warmth

painful hesitations
welcomed in full sun.

May dew on grass
be honoured
for its chill

slide a cool watering

dissipate in air,

sacred in passing.

Embrace
what you've got

open your rigid heart
to frail beauty,

the awkward small.

Little berries
in grubby hands

may we laugh
in tiny offerings,

drop our need for more.

These monkeys
preening,
grooming each other
foraging bugs in fur

threatening
with toothy grins

scrambling to eat
all day

wounding
and avoiding wounds

sometimes still
to hear wind
for a while

leaving a legacy,
shit for new trees

…not metaphor.

That church
tried to stop time

marking a calendar
to create a false start

there is no real thing
as a negative number

even after
and before

are only partial truths

let me sink into the timestream

where millions of yesterdays
and unseen tomorrows
are right here
in my belly.

Strawberry flowers
wild and delicate
tiny on the path

may result in teensy fruit
or not even

echo of someday
in their petals

a collective tumble
briefly beautiful.

Every hour this choice

to welcome who I am
just like this

without bliss
or torment

just a deep breath
saying hello

yet again.

I have tasted
bright joy

kinship with rusty nails
and delicate petals
and all my neighbours everywhere.

And so today
with its bare limbs
could feel like less

this poke of heart
remembering
what is not here now

let me fall
from this perch
as soon as I can

let wind
pry open my wings.

When the plane goes down
or death's staccato sounds
unpleasantly nearby

may some echo
of this humour
breed happy cousins

find a shimmer
on a cheekbone
still fleshed in

and riding a smile.

Let it be known
that this skeleton
loved dancing
in its bag of skin

and loved inviting others
to jiggle.

A stranger
in shape of friend
crossed a line
I'd traced invisibly
and so I made
ice cubes
slowly piled on sand

withdrawing my kindness.

Thank goodness
and again thank

how sun reveals shadow

how my little unfair walls

can drip away.

It is hard work
to be human

all these belly cramps
and tears

learning to birth
a good death

learning to give
everything away

even as we open our arms
to welcome it all

blowing tenderly
on embers
of delight.

Sun after rain
and our dog barking

joy in all this
imperfection

growth
for the sake of growing

DNA doing its thing.

And although I see for the first time
this reflection of a window

outside leaves shining
on a decorated wall

this perceiving
is by no means new.

It is time
to let wry humour glow

softening the grimaces
even as wounds
are peeled open

even as pus
is drained off

even as fatigue
makes us stumble

as we move
through meaningless days.

No problem
is a hard truth
to swallow comfortably

fierce kindness
in this medicine

to unhinge the mind

no ambrosia for escaping

whatever water is here.

The horse of my being
is snorting

stomping ground
in warning

shaking with fear.

O may I climb fences
extending my apple

welcome this frothing beast

ride myself gently

into wild unknown.

I am travelling
to see my teachers again

and feel homework undone

oil in my lamp
not brimming

reporting on a small world

instead of this lush planet
and its creeping deserts.

Apology and excuses
insufficient

second-string acolyte

feeling shame.

Sacred messenger
those delicate wings
moving so fast
seem invisible

graceful legs
buoyant in landing

a painless probe
inserted with precision

drawing forth
my lifeblood

in service to fertility.

And yes there is an itch
left in return

small offering of pain
in exchange
for priceless honouring.

            (for the Dalai Lama on behalf of
            mosquitoes)

Those bell flowers

magenta in sun

heads hanging down

otherwise

no sound can ring.

I was young
and her empty chair
jabbed my tears

today the sight of yours
so often full
provoked the same upwelling.

May I dance tenderly
with tomorrow,
not striving to see
his hidden face,

feeling his arms
and enough space
for breathing

feeling my feet
moving on ground.

My sons won't remember
the video store
with its red door in the back

yesterday's tech

but now I need
courage

let my soul
press the buzzer
even with others watching

to enter despite fear
the room of lust

ugly scenes of pain

vacuous boobs
bouncing for cash

dropping my aversions
even as I
reject falsehood

wander through
tits and titles
that scare me

bringing peace
in a life
with open doors.

Zeitgeist
flows so fast

our deep unseen

synapses outside flesh

my own ideas

already old

may gratitude
part my lips.

In my dream
I slapped a boy
to make him behave

and yes that's me
hitting me

the aggressor I deny.

Simpler to notice
my panic

and own my palm
wide open

slap tool

and also instrument of grace.

My pelvic bowl
like vodka
lit with blue flame

sweet fire
dangerous
this fear of causing harm
now burning

exquisite

this suckling
my own heat

impossible desire
to quench my thirst

igniting
the unseen web
contact
intense and fleeting.

That alley cat
has put away her claws

she pads now
with softer beauty,
licking her paws
and patching others
all day

learning to be stroked
without bristling

licking her lips
as if she swallowed a canary

and it still sings.

Staggering with stuff
she clanks
down the stairs

an act of discipline
and desperation

bereft of intention.

Sweet birdsong
plaintive on blue sky

summons her
to drop everything

no names

cathedral of now.

She wants the lichen
to cushion her ear
and whisper the words

the slowed undulation
of ridge line
to quiet her pace

a stillness of rock
moving her pen

a deepness of time

with each breath
a surfboard made of stone

riding an unseen wave
spoken by mountain.

It calls
her nameless name
and she's going.

In the fat
nausea

of defeat

surrendering
to quiet pains
accumulated sediments

may I give in
to shifting

feel compressed sand
dry clay

what I thought bedrock
moving

my nose in dust

heart damp
in open ribcage

unpleasantly alive

and still.

May the next few minutes
be fully lived

an offering
of deep noticing

awake to see
how impossible
this beauty

how unlikely
this interweaving

gaia mat
of space and time
connecting in bird calls

rich diversity of perches
for butterflies

idioms of insects
almost inaudible

helicopter like timpani
this symphony.

Thank you
innate goodness

for being here
all the time

even when I eclipse you
like a moon blocking light

my inevitable orbit
creating darkness
briefly.

You are gravity
and corona

we hang suspended
even as we journey

carried tenderly
by dark void
in all directions.

Dancing these days
is more like
furtive bobbing

tight heart
in tighter muscles,

a practiced scurry.

May I find
more wiggle

listen so deeply
that music
does the work

carries me
shaking

in wider circles.

Healing now
and healing never
the truth is
nothing is lacking

even though
we are designed
to disagree

the flow of all we need
is right here now
and never all
we can imagine
and still we swim
and rest.

O my friends
who have gone

leaving their half-smiles
like flickers on the wall

or inside my eyelids
after I have seen

may my sadness
draw me onwards
into this deep lap

the inbreath
of our first daylight

exhaling my release

a tender sorrow
of love recognized

reclaimed
after departure

absorbed
in these buzzing cells.

Axis of reverence,
how the planet
tips

gently placing
dawn's arrival
somewhere new
each day

slow genuflection of seasons
bowing to the sun

inner sense
of when to change

an equinox of limit

defining a broad east
in a swath of north and south;

this patient journey,

my own deep nod.

Delighting in strangers

I marvel at all these smiles,

wealth piling itself

ephemeral grins.

And though a knock

used to bring my wince

now appreciation

propels my answer.

Spitting porcupine
my teen
bristling with fury

demanding solitude
for angry tears;

let me feel
my armour

and let it slide,

respect his
door

and close it gently
on my soft exit

feel the ouch
without fear.

This home
cracking open

comings and goings

sunlight
fading upholstery
nourishing perennials
including weeds

dizziness of freedom
and nausea of choice

may I cry
and cry again

creating mud from sand
moving it
into new shapes

laugh kindly
mud pies to share.

We all sing
these soft descants

soaring above
and below
the audible

our mouths so rarely open

our ears so often filled
with other sounds

each
unspoken melody
so beautiful.

This greed
of wanting

joy, and kindness

health, and fluid wellbeing

clarity of heart and eyes,

a tidy desk

a passionate bed

a contagious smile...

may the earthquake
rumble through me

change direction
of my flow

surprise the engineers

when water flows upstream

overtaking the dam.

I have no more time

to wait patiently

for safety

this power

deeply threatening

all I know

to have been true

opening
all these false constraints

wind through a haystack
built with care

flying and falling.

No one wants their nose
held down to ground,
pushed towards defeat
by someone's harsh foot

nor the glare
from stark mirrors
and cruel judgments

but oh! the brave ones know
indignity
as prostration on the precious earth

and the truth
of winter light
turning to spring.

I walked down a hill
bathing in light
shining from outside and in

and saw a man in shadows.

Instead of my usual smile
delivered with a wince

I planned a good morning
for his brown Latino head.

Imagine my wonder
to see his green eyes and skin,
to hear his frog voice
gravelly in reply

and feel his touch,
a fingertip
of all I do not understand.

Three women
belly
heart
mind

travelling together
with different gifts

birthing
loving
paying attention

listening to all three
in each one

complex simplicity

refracting one journey

in tears that glisten.

Let my body

heal itself

let my heart

crack itself open

sprouting out my back

with feathers

leaving trails I cannot see

let kindness
fill today with ease
like a hot bath
with no taps

may I deeply give away
all pretence

enjoy my invisible nature

a soft and formless breeze.

Divine love
flows through all

in hiding
under farts
and unkind texting

delivered with care
through egos hard at work,

sliding under barricades
we each build every day.

These real lives
constrained
by allergies
or past trauma,
limping from blisters
or missing limbs

hobble
with awkward grace.

Your song

tossed like a ball

by a stranger in a park

enters my heart,

a playful gift

to pass along.

Make your offerings
now

polish or grind them
ink or rubber gloves
cinnamon or Twitter
hand outstretched

ego prostrate

joy in the face of danger.

Create your best
today

and the fullness of time

will prompt you

where to lay them down.

This quiet sculpting
is all about release

relinquishing
the cherished shapes

opening to new alignment
unfamiliar

balance
that feels odd

being clay

even as I flutter
these hands.

Summoned
to the itchy state

rise from slumber
to feel your thirst

your own pain
damned uncomfortable

and the agony
of our planet on fire.

Wake to the joy of feeling,

to the trust

that water will find you,

to the splash of your shaking hands

making mistakes

as you pour out for others.

I will never dance
in an owl costume
at the edge of a faraway cliff

and even say no
to trust falls
in a warm circle

and struggle as a passenger.

My courage fails me
often

yet still I keep travelling

to new edges

and call you to meet me
where you don't want to go

finding kindness there

and celebration.

Two women walking
boreal forest

before leaves
dead needles

one feeling pierced
by memory

one noticing light
playing with shadow

and then silence
shifted

trees looked more real

memory moved back to fringe

one woman walking.

These tight muscles
warning danger

are using fuel
I can recapture.

Let me drop
kindness
like a feeding tube

onto my fear

and then suck
my own heat

sustain
my forward motion.

The elder
with her grin
moving bravely
towards decrepitude

joyful
at the sight of husks

mature corn
peeping

shucking herself

to reveal
a wizened heart

a necessary shriveling,

sustaining nourishment

available,

fodder on offer.

What if you could listen
so intently

you heard the magic words

soundings bathing your belly
in a warm love

spreading your fearless smile

a blanket for sharing

a banner for journeying forwards

your mind translating firmly

a triumphant yes.

You'll never know
how life moves through you
to touch others

how your glance
on a street
changes lives

how your email
prods an action

how your crazy trust
in a wild oath

moves someone else
to greatness

or your silence
means they never hear
their next clue.

I feel my teacher
calling me home

this refracted path
she glints

myriad eyes
of wisdom

calling me
to a disillusioned
devotion

honouring
this powerful fragility

composite glimpses

demanding my reverence

gently pruning

this wild garden.

Sometimes all you have
is a tall tree
no leaves
barren arms stretching to sky

and another kind
in front
laden with blossoms

and how the sun shines
on them both

and they stand together
still.

Enough!

I hear command
in my voice,
shaking my mind
to drop tenacious drivel

and also hear entreaty,
the way I beg life
to provide

the way I beg myself
to find contentment.

May enough
be enough

may I stop scratching
and learn from the itch

may my hands fall open
to give and receive.

Muscles and molecules,
this collection of moments
needs no name

has had several
within recent memory

exchanges chemicals
with the planet
all day long

carries thousands of other lives
like a barnacled whale

these organisms moving together
experiencing flow,
digesting
what is here.

Some thoughts
are leeches

I swim in night water
and they find me

sucking my life
gently
but all day long.

I didn't even see them
in the rush

but now they are fatter
and I am growing pale

... time for salt
and awkward pain

letting them go
even though there will be
scars revealed

restoring my flow.

To enjoy
the dirty floor

poised between
memory and promise

it will shine again

like sun dancing with cloud.

To enjoy
the painful breath

with similar freedom

yesterday and tomorrow

like roots underground

nourishing
this rustling stillness.

I'm afraid
of my weirdness

fear my own re-naming
as Parakeet
or Mountain Echo

fear I will decorate
a shopping cart
and mumble in the streets

fear I will paw at strangers
and bind wounds
and cause others.

Let this fear of shame
stop riding my back

let me bounce
with open heart
into what is here.

My foot in the door
it's uncomfortable
to feel the squeeze

the weight of what keeps me
shut

and yet
warm light

wafts through this crack.

I will lean in,
add more heft to my desire

more yearning
to oil hinges

more of me
falling
to centre.

This kindness
like a thread
piercing my life
in the middle

the beads of my days
bumping
when I forget to feel

may I keep sinking
into the centre
of this filament

the vibrant delicate

the hollow tube

feel the glow
below understanding

connecting
these fine baubles

body and soul.

I give up again.

May these good intentions
and this pen

swirl away in surrender,

may I sink
in solidarity with despair
and all this awe

find courage
in the empty holes
of hopeless uncertainty

take refuge
in the welcome
of all these brave souls
with no clue

who embrace all this sorrow
with kindness

trail warm fingers
and dance in rubble.

www.ingramcontent.com/pod-product-compliance
Lightning Source LLC
Chambersburg PA
CBHW071830020426
42331CB00007B/1673